Th

An

Written by Quentin Flynn

Illustrated by Ian Forss

Contents Page

Nelson

an International Thomson Publishing company I(T)P®

The MacGregors And MacDougalls

With these characters ...

Griffin MacGregor

Des MacDougall

Gerry MacGregor

Ivan Inverness

Douglas MacDougall

"It had all begu

Setting the scene ...

For three hundred long years, the MacGregor family and the MacDougall family have been arguing. It all started with a wall being accidentally built in the wrong place and, ever since then, fathers and sons from both families have been behaving badly!

When Ivan Inverness, the principal of Killarnoch school, decides that the arguing must stop, he decides to try an unusual punishment to make the two youngest members of the families work together. Even Ivan doesn't think that his scheme will work: but there are surprising results in store for the MacGregors and the MacDougalls!

ne foggy morning in 1699 ..."

Chapter 1.

Ivan Inverness, the principal of Killarnoch Primary School, paced up and down behind his desk. His bushy white eyebrows curved down and met in the middle of his forehead, as he thought about the problem he faced.

Behind Ivan Inverness, the walls were covered with old photographs of all the classes that had been at Killarnoch Primary School for the last hundred years. His desk was piled high with papers, books and letters. His eyes settled on two nervous schoolboys, staring at the floor and fidgeting, in front of his desk.

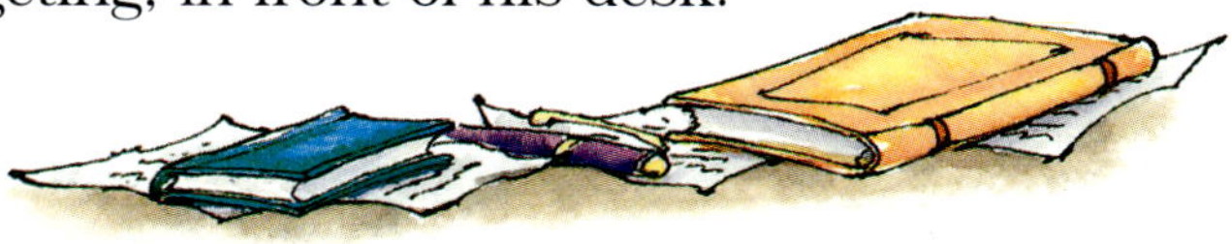

"Once more, you are in deep trouble, Griffin MacGregor," growled Ivan Inverness finally. Griffin, the smaller of the two boys, squirmed in his chair. The other boy nudged him in the ribs, and pulled a face, until the principal spoke to him as well. "And don't think that you will get away with this either, Des MacDougall."

Ivan Inverness's eyebrows moved like a long, hairy caterpillar as he spoke firmly. "You are *both* in deep trouble."

"But it was that sneak Griffin who *put* the worm in my sandwich!" protested Des, in a voice as big and rough as he looked. "He started it, so *he* should be punished."

"Don't interrupt! It was *you* who forced Griffin to *eat* the sandwich," replied the principal grimly.

Griffin bit his bottom lip and grimaced, as he remembered the taste of the worm. Des put his hands over his mouth to hide a big smirk.

Ivan Inverness sighed. Ever since he had been at Killarnoch Primary School, this had been a recurring problem. The MacGregors and the MacDougalls simply could not get along. He stared at an old photograph from 1965, and focused on the young faces of the boys' fathers, Gerry MacGregor and Douglas MacDougall. In 1965, Ivan's first year as principal of Killarnoch, both Gerry and Douglas looked exactly like their sons. Ivan sighed again.

Even the boys' fathers had fought at school, he remembered. Just as the boys' grandfathers had fought, too, when Ivan was a boy in their class. In fact, it had been the same problem for three hundred years.

Ivan Inverness folded his arms, having finally thought of a punishment.

"Griffin, you will help Des with his homework for a week. Des, you will help Griffin with his football practice for a week. That way, you may learn that each of you has different strengths, and that you should use them to help each other, not to hinder each other."

Ivan Inverness secretly thought it was highly unlikely that the two boys would learn *anything*, but it was the best solution he could think of. There was only one term left of the school year, and then both Des and Griffin would leave to go to high school. He might get some peace at his school for the last term—but he wouldn't be surprised if there was no peace between the MacGregors and the MacDougalls for another three hundred years.

The boys glared at each other.

"It's not fair," they both complained.

"Well, I'm glad you agree on at least *one* thing," retorted their principal. "Now hurry back to class. And behave yourselves!"

Chapter 2.

"You hid a worm in Des MacDougall's sandwich?" chuckled Griffin MacGregor's father, Gerry. "That's my clever boy," he beamed proudly. "Well done!"

"Don't encourage him," warned his mother, Emily. "You should be setting an example by ending the feud between our families."

“You’re right, my dear,” nodded Gerry. He turned back to his son. “Did I ever tell you about the time I hid a mouse in Douglas MacDougall’s lunch box? Now, that was a sight to see! That big, hairy oaf almost fell off his chair when the mouse leapt out at him at lunchtime! Ha ha ha!”

Griffin listened intently as his father told him all the hilarious tricks he had played on his enemy when he was at school. Emily MacGregor decided to ignore her husband, and noisily turned the pages of her newspaper. She could still hear the occasional words, however: “prank”, “beetle milkshake” and “dumb-dumb”.

Over at the MacDougall house, Douglas MacDougall was clapping his son on the shoulder.

"Excellent, my boy," he was saying loudly. "Forcing that MacGregor boy to eat a worm sandwich? This boy's turning out to be a real MacDougall!"

"Oh, Douglas, do shut up!" said his wife, Hettie, angrily.

"Did I ever tell you about the time I forced Gerry MacGregor to eat a whole box of plums one lunchtime? He was on the toilet for the next three days!" Douglas MacDougall's moustache waggled as he roared with laughter. He was delighted that his son was keeping the family feud alive.

The families' feuding had begun one foggy morning in 1699. Des MacDougall's great-great-great-great-grandpa, Lachlan MacDougall, was carefully pegging out a string line. He was building a new stone wall along the border of his land and the MacGregor farm.

Thomas and Gracie MacGregor, and Doris MacDougall, went out in the evening to see Lachlan's work.

"Looks good to me," enthused Thomas.

"My sons and I will start building tomorrow," Lachlan replied.

That night, while they were sleeping, one of Thomas MacGregor's goats, Milly, wandered from her pen. She found Lachlan's left-over lunch by a whortleberry bush, beside the wall-to-be. She ate it in one gulp.

On her way home, Milly snagged her leg on the string line. She pulled the line forwards and backwards until she untangled herself. But there was a whole goat-length added to the MacDougall farm after Milly had pulled the string this way and that way.

Next morning, the muscular MacDougalls worked hard, stacking the stones to fit perfectly along the line of the string. They worked for weeks. Thomas and Gracie watched from their upstairs window as the wall took shape.

At last, when the wall was finished, both families met for a picnic.

As he sat admiring the wall, Thomas noticed something odd. The whortleberry bush that was usually on his farm now stood on the other side of the wall. Of course, no-one knew about Milly's night-time wandering, and so the feud began.

Thomas MacGregor accused the MacDougalls of deliberately stealing his land. "You cheat, MacDougall!" he shouted.

Lachlan MacDougall was terribly offended. "You could have helped build the wall, you puny wimp!" he yelled back.

The two families would not talk to each other from that day on. Until Ivan Inverness intervened ...

Chapter 3.

The next day, Griffin MacGregor trudged out to the football field. He always felt he was too small to play football well. And he *especially* didn't like the idea of football practice with Des MacDougall. At the other end of the field stood Des, bouncing the ball with an evil smirk on his face.

"Come on, Griffin," yelled Des impatiently. He wheeled around and kicked the ball ferociously into the goal. The net stretched with the force of Des's shot.

When the ball rolled back to Des, he kicked the ball straight at Griffin.

Thump! The ball hit Griffin right in the chest, and nearly knocked him over. Des ran up to him and dribbled the ball round and round Griffin, before kicking it at him again. Thump! This time, it hit Griffin on the shoulder.

"Kick it back, you measly MacGregor," yelled Des. He kicked it again, and Griffin tried to duck. Now he was becoming angry. This was not fair! After all, *he* was the one who had been forced to eat the worm sandwich. And now he would be black and blue all over, with bruises from the football.

"Like this?" asked Griffin. "I'll get you back *harder*," he thought angrily. He put all his might into a huge kick, straight at his enemy.

The ball curved around Des at high speed, and slammed into the goal. Des MacDougall looked surprised.

"Lucky shot," he sulked, as he fetched the ball. "Bet you can't do that again!"

Griffin was furious. He wanted to kick the ball straight at Des's head. But he missed again, and the ball whistled past Des MacDougall's left ear, and thumped into the goal.

Des didn't say anything, but he looked amazed. He dribbled the ball up to Griffin, and tried to get past him. But Griffin was smaller and faster, and flicked the ball out from underneath Des's feet. Des pushed him out of the way, and took the ball back. He spun around and was about to shoot for goal himself, just to show this MacGregor that it was easy, anyway.

But Griffin stood in the way, and the ball bounced off his head.

Des was about to laugh, until he saw where the ball had bounced. It rolled into the goal.

"Wow," he whispered. "That was a good header!"

After school, both boys had to stay behind for an hour, so that Griffin could help Des with his maths homework.

Des stared at the graph paper in front of him. His eyes glazed over. He hated maths. He didn't understand it at all. Anyway, what use was maths going to be?

They were studying sets and Venn diagrams.

"It's easy," said Griffin, sighing and rolling his eyes. Des looked at the two sets in front of him. Numbers surrounded by circles. What was that supposed to mean?

"Think of them as two groups of people. This can be your family," said Griffin, pointing at one set of numbers. "And this can be my family," he said, pointing at the other.

Then he drew the two circles so they overlapped. There were two numbers in the part where both circles overlapped.

"These two numbers are in both circles. Think of them as the only MacGregor and the only MacDougall to talk to each other," explained Griffin.

Des chewed on the end of his pencil. He was puzzled.

"But no-one in our families talks to each other," he said.

"We do," said Griffin. Slowly, Des stopped looking bored and chewing his pencil.

"So," he said hesitantly, "these are the sneaky numbers and these are the strong numbers?"

Griffin sighed, and flopped back in his chair. Des was on the right track, but this was going to be a long hour!

Ivan Inverness, the principal, peered in through the classroom window. His caterpillar eyebrows curled, as he saw the two boys huddled together.

"Well, well," he said to himself. "I never thought I'd see the day when a MacGregor and a MacDougall would work together without a fight."

Chapter 4.

At the salmon-canning factory where both boys' fathers worked, machinery hissed and clattered as the cans of salmon were filled and sealed. Gerry MacGregor stood at one end of the factory line, and Douglas MacDougall stood at the other end. They never spoke to each other.

Gerry MacGregor turned to the factory worker next to him, and nudged her.

"My boy Griffin is teaching that great hairy oaf's boy to do maths," he sniggered. "Have you ever heard anything so ridiculous?"

Douglas MacDougall looked up and glared at Gerry MacGregor.

"Those MacDougalls are so dumb they have to count all their fingers at the end of the day to remind themselves how many toes they have!" laughed Gerry heartily. "And even then, they have to do it twice to make sure they're right." He giggled again.

Douglas MacDougall turned to the factory worker next to him.

“My boy Des is teaching that little sneak’s boy to play football,” he guffawed. “Can you imagine that?”

Gerry MacGregor narrowed his eyes at Douglas MacDougall.

“The last time a MacGregor played football,” snorted Douglas, “we used him *as* the football! Even then, he was useless. He didn’t bounce very well at all!” Douglas laughed loudly, and pretended to kick an imaginary MacGregor around the floor.

Amazingly, after a week, both Des and Griffin were actually looking forward to maths homework and football practice.

"Let's start with triangles, rectangles and parallelograms," explained Griffin. Des eagerly brought out his graph paper and drew a perfect set of shapes.

"That's easy," he said proudly. "Let's move on to some more difficult maths."

After an hour of homework, Des showed Griffin how to kick the football backwards over his head. Griffin flicked the ball up into the air, and kicked a perfect goal over his head.

"Goal!" yelled Des excitedly. "Now try this shot." He showed Griffin another shot.

Even though the punishment week was over, Ivan Inverness was amazed to see that the boys still practiced football and did their homework together. He smiled to himself, as he peered out his window and saw Griffin and Des dribbling a football around and around each other.

"This really is the strangest thing," he said, shaking his head. "Who would have ever thought?"

Chapter 5.

At the end of the school year, there was a big prize-giving ceremony at Killarnoch Primary School. The parents and friends arrived and sat in the school hall. There was a murmur in the crowd as Ivan Inverness strode onto the stage.

"I'd like to welcome you all to the Killarnoch Millennium Prize-giving Ceremony," he said proudly. "We will start the prize-giving. And then, we have a few surprises."

Everyone looked at each other. What did he mean?

Ivan read out the list of prizewinners. First, he read out the winner of the English prize, followed by the winner of the arts prize. Then, he read out the winner of the social studies prize. All the students collected their prizes to the sound of people clapping enthusiastically.

At the end of the ceremony, Ivan raised his hands for silence.

"And now," he said, beaming, "we have two special prizes."

"For the most improved maths student," he said, looking around the hall. "The prize goes to ..."

Gerry MacGregor nudged his wife, Emily. "It'll be Griffin, for sure," he said, sitting up proudly, and getting ready to clap.

Ivan looked at his notes.

"Des MacDougall!"

There was a shocked silence in the hall. No-one looked more shocked than Gerry MacGregor. Except, perhaps, Douglas MacDougall. He stared at his wife, Hettie.

"Did I hear right? A maths prize?"

But Hettie just stood up and cheered. Everyone else in the hall stood up, too, and started to clap loudly. Des MacDougall walked proudly on stage, and waved at the crowd. Ivan handed him the prize, a new compass, and then he cleared his throat.

"Ahem," he said. "And now for the other special prize of the evening—the most improved sports player."

Douglas MacDougall sat up straight. "Des is about to get two prizes," he whispered excitedly to Hettie. "That'll annoy those sneaky MacGregors."

"Griffin MacGregor!" smiled Ivan Inverness.

Gerry MacGregor's mouth dropped open. He stared at his wife, but Emily was already on her feet, clapping and cheering. "Go, Griffin!" she was yelling. The people were clapping and cheering wildly.

Griffin walked proudly onto the stage and collected his prize, a pair of football socks. Then he walked over to where Des was standing and shook his hand. Everyone clapped and cheered even louder. In three hundred years, no-one had seen anything like it. This was unbelievable—but true! A MacDougall had won a maths prize—and a MacGregor had won a sports prize!

Chapter 6.

The next morning, the factory workers were talking about the prize-giving ceremony. They couldn't wait until Gerry and Douglas arrived at work.

Both men trudged in, looking very pleased with themselves. But, instead of standing at opposite ends of the canning line, Gerry walked up to Douglas and gave him a nudge.

The other workers stopped. The machines hissed and clattered to a stop. Was there going to be a fight? Instead, Gerry smiled at Douglas.

"That was very nice of your boy to help Griffin," said Gerry to Douglas. "He's the first MacGregor to ever win a prize for sport. Old Ivan Inverness thinks he'll go on to play for Scotland one day," said Gerry proudly.

Douglas looked at Gerry, and smiled back at him.

"Well, Hettie and I were grateful that your boy helped Des," he said gruffly. "We've never had a maths prizewinner in our family. Inverness says if Des keeps studying, he'll earn a scholarship to university."

Everyone at the factory stared, as the two men settled down to work, side by side. No-one could ever remember a MacGregor and a MacDougall working side by side before—not in a hundred years of canning salmon in Killarnoch.

Even more amazing was that, during their lunch break, Douglas MacDougall sat down next to Gerry MacGregor. The lunch room fell silent, as the other factory workers wondered what would happen next. This was a most peculiar day.

"Maybe it's time we stopped fighting," said Douglas, leaning over to Gerry.

"Maybe," agreed Gerry. There was an awkward silence for a few seconds. Then Gerry spoke again.

"Would you like to share a sandwich?"

No-one in the lunch room was more amazed than Douglas, but he smiled graciously and nodded. Gerry held out his lunch box and flipped open the lid.

Suddenly, the silence in the lunch room was shattered as Douglas MacDougall let out a huge scream, and toppled backwards off his chair. A tiny grey mouse leapt out of the lunch box and skittered across the floor.

"You great hairy oaf!" laughed Gerry. "At last! I've been wanting to make you fall off your chair for thirty years!"

Douglas MacDougall frowned and started to make a furious face. But then, as he looked up and saw the tears of laughter rolling down his old enemy's face, his anger dissolved into laughter, too. He picked himself off the floor and nudged Gerry in the ribs.

"I'll bring lunch tomorrow," he boomed, in between gasping for air. "I've got a nice box of plums sitting at home, and I remember just how much you like plums."

After three hundred years, the MacGregors and the MacDougalls had finally stopped fighting. And back in his principal's office, Ivan Inverness sat with a smile on his face. He looked up at the newest photograph on his wall—the class of '99. It was the only photograph in sight where a MacGregor and a MacDougall were standing next to each other, with big smiles on their faces.

He somehow knew it wouldn't be the last.

"Now, if only I can think of a way to stop the McMahons and the MacDonalds bickering. And the MacLeods and the McLachlans."

He shook his head, and smiled. He wondered what the photograph of the class of 2000 would look like.

"One trick more!"

For three hundred years and more,
Two feuding clans have been at war.

One side wiry, one side strong,
Both sides silly, both sides wrong.

There seems no answer to this mess!
Each family bent on more distress!

Then with a principal's persuasion,
Football practice and maths equations,

Two sons do stop the families' fight,
With surprise results on prize-giving night.

Two fathers, proud and pleased as punch,
Do sit together to share their lunch.

There is, however, a surprise in store ...
A final chance for one trick more!